The Ultimate Mongolia Travel Guide

Plan Your Dream Trip To Mongolia With
Insider Tips, Practical Advice, And
Inspiring Itineraries

Richard Bautista

INTRODUCTION

INTRODUCTION

Mongolia, a landlocked country nestled between Russia and China, is a land of vast deserts, rugged mountains, and rolling grasslands. It's a country where the nomadic way of life still prevails, and where the sky seems to stretch on forever. If you're looking for a unique travel experience, Mongolia is a destination that should be at the top of your list.

This Ultimate Mongolia Travel Guide is designed to help you plan your perfect trip to this magnificent country. Whether you're a seasoned traveler or a first-time visitor, this guide has everything you need to know to make the most of your time in Mongolia.

In this guide, you'll find information on the country's history and culture, its stunning natural landscapes, and the best ways to get around. You'll learn about the different regions of Mongolia and what they have to offer, from the bustling capital city of Ulaanbaatar to the serene beauty of Lake Khovsgol.

We'll also provide you with practical tips and advice to help you navigate the challenges of traveling in Mongolia. From choosing the right accommodation to understanding the local customs, this guide has got you covered.

But this guide is more than just a list of facts and figures. We'll take you on a journey through the heart of Mongolia, introducing you to the people, places, and experiences that make this country so special. You'll learn about the traditional Mongolian way of life, sample the local cuisine, and discover the hidden gems that only the locals know about.

So if you're ready to embark on an adventure like no other, join us as we explore the wonders of Mongolia. This Ultimate Mongolia Travel Guide is your passport to an unforgettable journey through one of the world's most unique and captivating destinations.

CHAPTER ONE

DISCOVERING MONGOLIA'S HISTORY AND CULTURE

Mongolia's history is a complex and fascinating tapestry of nomadic tribes, powerful empires, and political upheaval. From the early nomadic civilizations to the present day, Mongolia has undergone significant changes, yet it remains a proud and fiercely independent country with a rich cultural heritage.

Early History of Mongolia

The earliest inhabitants of Mongolia were nomadic tribes, who roamed the vast grasslands that make up much of the country. These tribes lived in portable tents called gers and relied on horses, sheep, and cattle for their livelihoods. The nomads developed a unique culture and way of life, which would continue to be an important part of Mongolian identity to this day.

In the 13th century, the legendary Genghis Khan united the nomadic tribes of Mongolia and established the Mongol

Empire, one of the largest empires in history. Under Genghis Khan's leadership, the Mongols conquered much of Asia, Europe, and the Middle East, leaving a lasting impact on world history.

Mongolian Buddhism

In the 16th century, Mongolia became a stronghold of Tibetan Buddhism, which remains the dominant religion in the country to this day. The religion played a significant role in shaping Mongolian culture and society, with monasteries and temples becoming centers of learning and artistic expression.

During the Soviet era, the Mongolian Communist Party implemented policies that sought to suppress religion and traditional culture. Many monasteries were destroyed, and religious leaders were persecuted. However, since the fall of communism in 1990, Buddhism has experienced a revival, and many of the country's historic monasteries have been restored.

Modern Mongolia

Since the fall of communism, Mongolia has undergone significant changes, both economically and politically. The country has embraced democracy, and its economy has grown rapidly, thanks in part to the country's vast mineral resources.

Despite these changes, Mongolia remains a country steeped in tradition and culture. The nomadic way of life still prevails in many parts of the country, and the herding of livestock remains a vital part of the economy. Mongolia is also known for its traditional arts and crafts, including intricate textiles and stunning metalwork.

Preserving Mongolia's Culture

In recent years, there has been a renewed focus on preserving Mongolia's unique cultural heritage. The government has established programs to promote the study and preservation of traditional Mongolian music, dance, and art. Efforts are also underway to preserve Mongolia's historic sites and monuments, such as the ancient city of Karakorum and the stunning Erdene Zuu Monastery.

In conclusion, Mongolia's history and culture are as diverse and complex as the country's stunning landscapes. From the early nomadic tribes to the powerful Mongol Empire and the rise of Buddhism, Mongolia has a rich and fascinating past that has shaped its identity to this day. As the country continues to evolve, it remains committed to preserving its traditions and cultural heritage, making Mongolia a unique and captivating destination for travelers.

CHAPTER TWO

EXPLORING MONGOLIA'S NATURAL WONDERS

Mongolia is a landlocked country located in East Asia, with an area of 1.56 million square kilometers. The country has a diverse landscape, ranging from mountains and deserts to grasslands and forests. Its natural wonders are a testament to the beauty and diversity of nature.

Gobi Desert

The Gobi Desert is one of the most famous natural wonders in Mongolia. It is a vast desert covering over 500,000 square miles and stretches across Mongolia and China. The desert is home to a variety of unique wildlife, including Bactrian camels, desert foxes, and the endangered Gobi bear.

Khuvsgul Lake

Khuvsgul Lake is a freshwater lake located in northern Mongolia near the Russian border. The lake is the second-largest freshwater lake in Asia and is surrounded by stunning mountain ranges. The lake is also home to a variety of fish species, including the endemic Hovsgol grayling.

Orkhon Waterfall

The Orkhon Waterfall is located in central Mongolia and is one of the country's most famous natural wonders. The waterfall is over 20 meters high and is surrounded by stunning landscapes, including the Orkhon Valley, which is a UNESCO World Heritage Site.

Altai Mountains

The Altai Mountains are a mountain range located in western Mongolia. The mountains are home to a variety of unique wildlife, including the snow leopard, ibex, and argali sheep. The area is also famous for its stunning landscapes, including the Tsambagarav Uul National Park and the Tavan Bogd National Park.

Bayanzag

Bayanzag, also known as the *"Flaming Cliffs,"* is located in southern Mongolia and is famous for its unique rock formations and red sandstone cliffs. The area is also home to a variety of dinosaur fossils, including the famous Velociraptor.

Khorgo-Terkhiin Tsagaan Lake National Park

The Khorgo-Terkhiin Tsagaan Lake National Park is located in central Mongolia and is home to a variety of unique landscapes, including volcanic craters, hot springs, and the stunning Terkhiin Tsagaan Lake. The area is also home to a variety of wildlife, including the Siberian ibex and the endangered snow leopard.

Khustain Nuruu National Park

Khustain Nuruu National Park is located in central Mongolia and is home to the endangered Przewalski's horse, also known as the Mongolian wild horse. The park is also home to a variety of other wildlife, including the Mongolian gazelle, argali sheep, and gray wolf. The park's landscapes include grassy steppe and forested mountains.

Yol Valley

Yol Valley, also known as the Eagle Valley, is located in southern Mongolia within the Gobi Gurvansaikhan National Park. The valley is known for its deep canyon and towering cliffs that shelter a small stream that freezes in winter, creating a natural ice tunnel that remains frozen even in summer. The valley is also home to unique wildlife, including the bearded vulture and the Gobi ibex.

Khongor Sand Dunes

Khongor Sand Dunes are located in southern Mongolia and are known for their massive size, reaching up to 300 meters in height. The dunes stretch for over 180 kilometers and are home to unique wildlife, including the long-eared jerboa and the Gobi desert frog. The dunes are also popular for camel riding and sandboarding.

Ulaanbaatar City

Ulaanbaatar is the capital city of Mongolia and is home to a variety of cultural and natural attractions. The city is surrounded by mountains, including the Bogd Khan Mountain National Park, which offers stunning views of the city and is home to a variety of unique wildlife. The city also has several museums, including the National Museum of Mongolia, which showcases the country's history and culture.

Mongolia offers a diverse range of natural wonders, from the vast Gobi Desert to the stunning Khuvsgul Lake and the unique Yol Valley. These natural wonders are home to a variety of unique wildlife, and visitors can also experience Mongolian culture and history in Ulaanbaatar. A trip to Mongolia is a must for anyone who loves nature and wants to experience the beauty and diversity of the natural world.

In conclusion, Mongolia's natural wonders offer a unique and diverse landscape that is home to a variety of unique wildlife and stunning landscapes. From the vast Gobi Desert to the stunning Khuvsgul Lake, Mongolia's natural wonders are testaments to the beauty of nature

CHAPTER THREE

PLANNING YOUR TRIP TO MONGOLIA

Mongolia is a vast country with a unique culture and landscape that is unlike anywhere else in the world. Planning a trip to Mongolia requires careful consideration of many factors, including when to go, what to see and do, and how to get around.

When to Visit Mongolia

The best time to visit Mongolia depends on what you want to see and do. The summer months of June through August are the most popular for travel, as the weather is warm, and the grasslands are lush and green. This is also the best time to witness the Naadam Festival, Mongolia's most famous cultural event.

If you are interested in winter activities such as skiing, dog sledding, and ice fishing, then the winter months of December through February are the best time to visit. However, be prepared for extremely cold temperatures, especially in the northern parts of the country.

What to See and Do in Mongolia

Mongolia is a country of vast, open spaces, and there is no shortage of things to see and do. Here are some of the must-see attractions and activities:

Explore the Gobi Desert

The Gobi Desert covers a vast area of southern Mongolia and is home to unique wildlife, such as the elusive snow leopard and the double-humped Bactrian camel.

Visit the Erdene Zuu Monastery

Located in the ancient city of Karakorum, the Erdene Zuu Monastery is one of the oldest and most important Buddhist monasteries in Mongolia.

Attend the Naadam Festival

Held every July, the Naadam Festival is a celebration of Mongolian culture and features traditional sports such as horse racing, wrestling, and archery.

Go horseback riding

Horseback riding is an essential part of Mongolian culture, and there are many opportunities to explore the country's vast grasslands on horseback.

Visit Lake Khovsgol

Lake Khovsgol is one of the largest and deepest freshwater lakes in Asia and is surrounded by stunning mountain scenery.

How to Get Around in Mongolia

Mongolia's vast size and rugged terrain make getting around the country a challenge. There are several options for transportation, depending on your budget and travel style:

Domestic Flights

There are several domestic airlines that operate flights between Ulaanbaatar and other major cities in Mongolia.

Overland Tours

Many tour operators offer overland tours of Mongolia, which typically involve traveling in a 4x4 vehicle and camping in tents.

Public Transportation

Public transportation in Mongolia consists of buses and shared taxis, which can be crowded and uncomfortable.

Horseback Riding

For a truly authentic Mongolian experience, consider traveling by horseback, either on a guided tour or by renting a horse and venturing out on your own.

In conclusion, Planning a Trip to Mongolia requires careful consideration of many factors, from the best time to visit to how to get around. With its unique culture and stunning landscapes, Mongolia is a destination that should be on every traveler's bucket list. Whether you want to explore the Gobi Desert, attend the Naadam Festival, or simply immerse yourself in the country's rich nomadic culture, there is something for everyone in Mongolia.

CHAPTER FOUR

GETTING AROUND IN MONGOLIA

Mongolia is a vast country with a sparse population and a diverse landscape, which can make getting around a bit challenging. However, with proper planning and information, it is possible to explore the country and enjoy its natural and cultural wonders. Here are some ways to get around in Mongolia:

Domestic Flights

Mongolia has several domestic airports, including in Ulaanbaatar, the capital city, and other major cities like Erdenet, Darkhan, and Khovd. Domestic flights are a quick and efficient way to travel long distances, especially if you want to explore the western or northern regions of the country.

Bus and Minivan

Buses and minibuses are the most common mode of transportation in Mongolia, and they connect most major cities and towns. Buses and minibuses are affordable and offer a great opportunity to experience Mongolian culture by interacting with locals. However, they can be crowded, and the quality of the vehicles can vary, so it is important to choose a reputable company.

Taxi and Ride-hailing Services

Taxis are available in most cities and towns in Mongolia, and they are a convenient way to travel short distances. Ride-hailing services like Uber and Bolt are also available in Ulaanbaatar, offering an affordable and reliable option for getting around the city.

Car Rental

Renting a car is a great way to explore Mongolia at your own pace, especially if you want to venture off the beaten path. However, driving in Mongolia can be challenging, with poorly maintained roads and unpredictable weather conditions. It is important to have experience driving in challenging conditions and to choose a reputable rental company.

Horse and Camel Riding

Horse and camel riding are traditional modes of transportation in Mongolia, and they offer a unique way to experience the country's vast and beautiful landscapes. Horse riding tours are available in most cities and towns, and camel riding is available in the Gobi Desert.

Cycling

Cycling is becoming increasingly popular in Mongolia, with several tour operators offering guided cycling tours. Cycling is a great way to explore the country's natural beauty and experience the local culture.

Train

Mongolia has a railway network connecting its major cities with neighboring countries, including China and Russia. Train travel in Mongolia is a unique experience, offering stunning views of the country's landscapes and an opportunity to interact with locals. There are several classes of trains, ranging from budget-friendly to luxury options.

Hitchhiking

Hitchhiking is a common way to get around in Mongolia, especially in rural areas. Locals are often willing to give rides to travelers, and hitchhiking can be a great way to interact with locals and experience their hospitality. However, hitchhiking can be risky, so it is important to take precautions and travel with a companion.

Walking

Walking is a great way to explore Mongolia's cities and towns and get a closer look at local life. Walking tours are available in Ulaanbaatar and other major cities, offering a chance to learn about Mongolian culture and history. Walking is also a great way to explore Mongolia's natural wonders, like the Gobi Desert and the Altai Mountains.

In conclusion, getting around in Mongolia offers a wide range of options to suit different travel styles and budgets. From train travel and domestic flights to hitchhiking and walking, there are many ways to explore Mongolia's unique landscapes and experience its rich culture. Whatever mode of transportation you choose be sure to research your options, plan ahead, and take the necessary precautions to stay safe and enjoy your travels in Mongolia.

Getting around in Mongolia requires proper planning and information. Domestic flights, buses, taxis, ride-hailing services, car rentals, horse and camel riding, and cycling are all available options for exploring the country's diverse landscape and rich culture. Whatever mode of transportation you choose, remember to stay safe, be respectful of local customs, and enjoy the unique experiences that Mongolia has to offer.

CHAPTER FIVE

CULTURAL ETIQUETTE IN MONGOLIA

Mongolia is a country with a rich cultural heritage, and visitors should be aware of the customs and etiquette when interacting with locals. Understanding these cultural norms can enhance your travel experience and show respect for the local people.

Greeting Customs

In Mongolia, it is customary to greet people with a bow, placing your hands on your chest. This gesture is called "zolgokh," which is a sign of respect. When greeting someone, it is also common to ask about their well-being, and it is polite to inquire about their family and business.

Dress Code

Mongolians take pride in their appearance and are generally conservative in their dress. It is best to dress modestly, especially when visiting religious sites and government buildings. Women should avoid wearing revealing clothing, such as shorts or tank tops. Men should wear long pants and a shirt with sleeves.

Gift Giving

Gift giving is an important part of Mongolian culture, and it is customary to bring a small gift when visiting someone's home. When giving a gift, it is polite to use both hands and present it with the right hand. Avoid giving sharp objects or clocks, as these are considered bad luck.

Table Manners

When dining with Mongolians, it is important to observe proper table manners. Meals are typically served family-style, and it is polite to wait for the host or eldest guest to begin eating before starting your meal. It is customary to eat with your right hand, as the left hand is considered unclean. Do not point with your chopsticks or leave them standing upright in your bowl, as this is considered rude.

Respect for Elders

Respect for elders is an essential part of Mongolian culture. When speaking with an elder, it is customary to address them with a formal title, such as "auntie" or "uncle." When entering a ger (a traditional Mongolian dwelling), it is polite to step over the threshold with your right foot first, as the left foot is considered unclean.

Religious Customs

Mongolia is a predominantly Buddhist country, and visitors should be respectful of the local religious customs. When visiting a Buddhist temple or monastery, it is important to remove your shoes before entering and to dress modestly. Avoid pointing your feet towards the altar or Buddha statues, as this is considered disrespectful.

By understanding and respecting the cultural norms and customs of Mongolia, visitors can have a more meaningful and rewarding travel experience. From greeting customs to table manners, respecting elders to religious customs, taking the time to learn about the cultural etiquette of Mongolia shows respect for the local people and their way of life

CHAPTER SIX

OUTDOOR ACTIVITIES IN MONGOLIA

Mongolia is a country with vast and rugged terrain, making it an ideal destination for outdoor enthusiasts. The country offers a range of activities that showcase its natural beauty and unique culture. In this chapter, we'll explore some of the best outdoor activities to experience in Mongolia.

Hiking and Trekking

Mongolia is home to several beautiful national parks, including Terelj National Park and Gorkhi-Terelj National Park, which offer excellent hiking and trekking opportunities. Visitors can explore rugged landscapes, rolling hills, and scenic valleys. The Altai Mountains in western Mongolia are another popular hiking destination, known for their stunning scenery and diverse wildlife.

Horseback Riding

Horseback riding is an essential part of Mongolian culture, and visitors can experience the thrill of riding across the vast steppes on horseback. There are several horse trekking routes across the country, including the Khentii Mountains, the Orkhon Valley, and the Gobi Desert. Visitors can also join local herders on horseback to experience the traditional way of life.

Camping and Glamping

Mongolia is known for its stunning natural beauty, and camping is an excellent way to experience it firsthand. Visitors can camp in national parks, wilderness areas, or with local nomadic families. For those looking for a more luxurious camping experience, glamping (or glamorous camping) options are available. These campsites offer comfortable accommodation, hot showers, and delicious meals, all while enjoying the stunning Mongolian scenery.

Fishing

Fishing is a popular pastime in Mongolia, with several lakes, rivers, and streams offering excellent fishing opportunities. The most popular fishing destinations include the Onon River, the Selenge River, and Lake Hovsgol.

Visitors can catch a variety of fish, including salmon, trout, and taimen.

Winter Activities

Mongolia's long, cold winters offer unique outdoor activities, including ice skating, ice fishing, and dog sledding. Visitors can also experience traditional winter sports like buuz khyalgaa (Mongolian ice hockey) and shagai (Mongolian version of curling). The Altai Mountains also offer excellent opportunities for skiing and snowboarding.

In conclusion, Mongolia is a paradise for outdoor enthusiasts, offering a range of activities that showcase the country's natural beauty and unique culture. From hiking and horseback riding to camping and fishing, visitors can experience the best of Mongolia's great outdoors. With its rugged terrain, stunning landscapes, and rich cultural heritage, Mongolia is a must-visit destination for adventure seekers.

CHAPTER SEVEN

EXPLORING ULAANBAATAR AND BEYOND

Ulaanbaatar, the capital city of Mongolia, is a vibrant and bustling metropolis that offers a unique blend of traditional and modern culture. While the city has much to offer in terms of museums, restaurants, and nightlife, there are also many exciting destinations beyond the city limits that are well worth exploring. Here are some ideas for exploring Ulaanbaatar and beyond:

Visit the Gandan Monastery

The Gandan Monastery is one of the most important religious sites in Mongolia and is located in the heart of Ulaanbaatar. The monastery is home to several temples and is the center of Mongolian Buddhism. Visitors can watch the daily rituals and ceremonies performed by the monks and learn about the history of Buddhism in Mongolia.

Explore the National Museum of Mongolia

The National Museum of Mongolia is located in Ulaanbaatar and offers a fascinating insight into the country's history and culture. The museum's exhibits cover everything from prehistoric times to the present day and include artifacts, traditional costumes, and artwork.

Discover the Choijin Lama Temple Museum

The Choijin Lama Temple Museum is a former Buddhist temple that has been converted into a museum. The museum is located in Ulaanbaatar and features a collection of religious artifacts, including intricate carvings and paintings. Visitors can learn about the history of the temple and the role of Buddhism in Mongolian culture.

Visit the Gorkhi-Terelj National Park

The Gorkhi-Terelj National Park is located just outside of Ulaanbaatar and offers stunning views of the Mongolian countryside. The park is home to several hiking trails, including one that leads to a rock formation known as the Turtle Rock. Visitors can also enjoy horseback riding, camping, and other outdoor activities.

Explore the Erdene Zuu Monastery

The Erdene Zuu Monastery is located in the town of Kharkhorin, about 240 kilometers west of Ulaanbaatar. The monastery is one of the oldest and most important religious sites in Mongolia and is a UNESCO World Heritage Site. Visitors can explore the monastery's temples, stupas, and other religious artifacts and learn about the history of Buddhism in Mongolia.

Visit the Khuvsgul Lake

The Khuvsgul Lake is located in northern Mongolia, about 700 kilometers from Ulaanbaatar. The lake is one of the largest freshwater lakes in the world and is surrounded by beautiful mountains and forests. Visitors can enjoy hiking, fishing, kayaking, and other outdoor activities, as well as experience the local culture of the nearby nomadic tribes.

In conclusion, exploring Ulaanbaatar and beyond offers a unique and exciting travel experience. From the city's religious and cultural landmarks to the natural wonders of the countryside, there is much to discover in Mongolia. Whether you choose to stay in Ulaanbaatar or venture further afield, be sure to take the time to learn about the local culture and customs and enjoy the hospitality of the Mongolian people.

CHAPTER EIGHT

EMBRACING MONGOLIAN HOSPITALITY AND CUISINE

Mongolian hospitality and cuisine are an integral part of the country's culture and history. The people of Mongolia are known for their warm and welcoming nature, and their cuisine reflects the country's nomadic heritage and love of meat and dairy products. Here are some tips for embracing Mongolian hospitality and cuisine during your travels:

Stay with a Local Family

One of the best ways to experience Mongolian hospitality is to stay with a local family. This is known as "ger homestay" and involves staying in a traditional Mongolian ger (yurt) and sharing meals and experiences with your hosts. Staying with a local family allows you to learn about Mongolian culture and customs firsthand and to experience the warmth and hospitality of the Mongolian people.

Try Traditional Mongolian Foods

Mongolian cuisine is heavily influenced by the country's nomadic heritage and is centered on meat and dairy products. Some popular dishes include buuz (steamed dumplings), khuushuur (fried meat pies), and tsuivan (stir-fried noodles). Mongolian cuisine also features a variety of dairy products, including airag (fermented mare's milk) and aaruul (dried curds). Be sure to try these traditional foods during your travels in Mongolia to experience the country's unique culinary culture.

Participate in a Mongolian Feast

Mongolian feasts, known as *"khorkhog,"* are a traditional way of celebrating special occasions and events. A khorkhog involves cooking meat, usually lamb or goat, with hot stones in a large pot until it is tender and juicy. The meat is then served with vegetables and other side dishes. Participating in a khorkhog is a great way to experience Mongolian hospitality and to celebrate with locals.

Learn about Mongolian Tea Culture

Mongolian tea culture is an important part of the country's social customs and hospitality. Tea is often served to guests as a gesture of welcome, and Mongolian tea ceremonies are a way of showing respect and gratitude. Mongolian tea is usually made with milk, salt, and sometimes butter or cheese, giving it a unique flavor. Learning about Mongolian tea culture and participating in a tea ceremony is a great way to experience the country's hospitality and customs.

Interact with Locals

Interacting with locals is one of the best ways to experience Mongolian hospitality. Mongolian people are known for their warm and welcoming nature, and they are often eager to share their culture and traditions with visitors. Whether you are staying with a local family, shopping at a market, or enjoying a meal at a restaurant, be sure to take the time to talk to locals and learn about their lives and experiences.

Attend a Naadam Festival

The Naadam Festival is the biggest and most important event in Mongolia, and it is a celebration of the country's nomadic heritage and traditional sports. The festival features three main events: wrestling, horse racing, and archery. Attending a Naadam Festival is a great way to experience Mongolian culture and hospitality, as the festival brings together people from all over the country and is a time of celebration and joy.

Visit a Nomadic Family

Mongolian nomads have a unique way of life that is centered on their herds of livestock and their traditional dwellings, known as gers. Visiting a nomadic family and learning about their way of life is a great way to experience Mongolian hospitality and to gain a deeper understanding of the country's culture and traditions. Many tour companies offer the opportunity to visit nomadic families and to learn about their daily lives.

Participate in a Shamanic Ceremony

Shamanism is an ancient spiritual tradition that is still practiced in Mongolia today. Shamanic ceremonies involve rituals and offerings to the spirits and ancestors, and they are a way of seeking guidance and protection. Participating in a shamanic ceremony is a unique way to experience Mongolian culture and to learn about the country's spiritual traditions.

Taste Mongolian Beverages

In addition to traditional Mongolian foods, the country also has a variety of unique beverages. Airag, mentioned earlier, is a popular drink made from fermented mare's milk. Mongolian beer is also gaining popularity, and there are several local breweries producing their own beers. Additionally, Mongolian vodka, known as "arkhi," is made from fermented milk and is a strong and potent drink. Trying these unique beverages is a great way to experience Mongolian culture and hospitality.

Learn Basic Mongolian Phrases

Finally, learning a few basic Mongolian phrases can go a long way in experiencing the country's hospitality. Simple phrases like *"hello"* (*"sain baina uu"*), *"thank you"* (*"bayarlalaa"*), and *"delicious"* (*"ungalaa"*) can help you connect with locals and show your appreciation for their hospitality and cuisine. Mongolian people are often impressed and delighted when visitors take the time to learn a few words of their language, so don't be afraid to try.

In conclusion, embracing Mongolian hospitality and cuisine is an important part of any trip to Mongolia. Whether you are staying with a local family, trying traditional Mongolian foods, participating in a khorkhog, learning about Mongolian tea culture, or interacting with locals, there are many ways to experience the warmth and generosity of the Mongolian people. Be sure to take the time to immerse yourself in the country's culture and traditions and to enjoy the hospitality and cuisine of this unique and fascinating destination.

Printed in Great Britain
by Amazon

23041883R00030